Simple Pleasures for
BUSY WOMEN

DIMENSIONS
FOR LIVING
NASHVILLE

Simple Pleasures for Busy Women

Copyright © 1996 by Dimensions for Living

All rights reserved.
No part of this work may be reproduced or transmitted in any form or by any means, electronic or mechanical, including photocopying and recording, or by any information service or retrieval system, except as may be expressly permitted by the 1976 Copyright Act or in writing from the publisher. Requests for permission should be addressed to Dimensions for Living, P.O. Box 801, 201 Eighth Avenue South, Nashville, TN 37202-0801.

This book is printed on recycled, acid-free paper.

ISBN 0-687-05550-4
CIP data available from the Library of Congress.

Scripture quotations noted KJV are from the King James Version of the Bible.

Those noted NIV are taken from the Holy Bible: New International Version. Copyright © 1973, 1978, 1984 by the International Bible Society. Used by permission of Zondervan Bible Publishers.

Those noted NRSV are from the New Revised Standard Bible, copyright © 1989 by the Division of Christian Education of the National Council of the Churches of Christ in the United States of America, and are used by permission.

96 97 98 99 00 01 02 03 04 05—10 9 8 7 6 5 4 3 2 1

MANUFACTURED IN THE UNITED STATES OF AMERICA

*You show me the path of life.
In your presence there is
fullness of joy;
in your right hand
are pleasures forevermore.*

—Psalm 16:11 NRSV

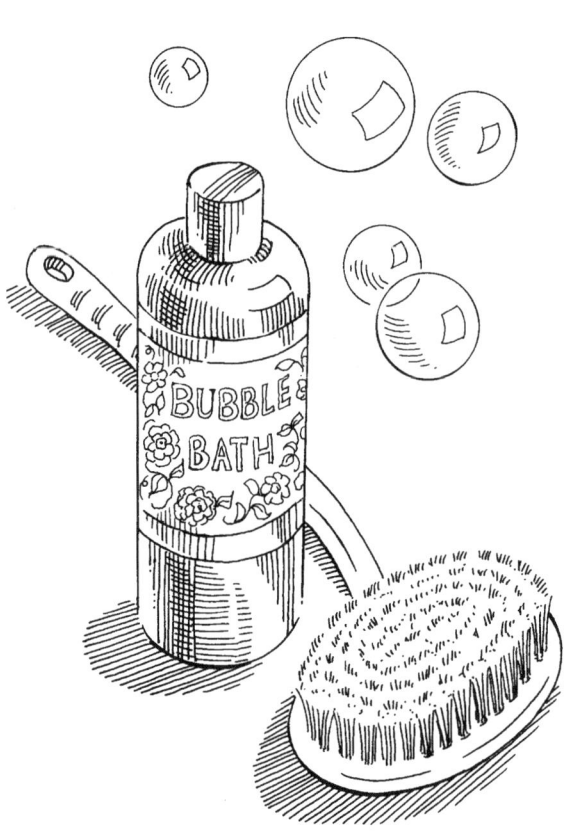

One

Take a bubble bath.

*I wash my hands in innocence,
and go around your altar, O LORD,
singing aloud a song of thanksgiving,
and telling all your wondrous deeds.*

—Psalm 26:6-7 NRSV

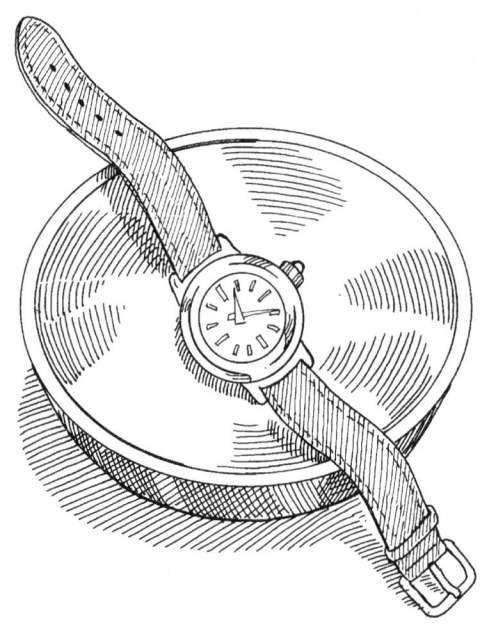

Two

Take off your watch for the weekend.

Six days thou shalt do thy work, and on the seventh day thou shalt rest.

—Exodus 23:12 KJV

Three

Get dressed up and listen to the symphony on the radio.

*Praise the L*ORD *with the lyre; make melody to him with the harp of ten strings.*

—Psalm 33:2 NRSV

Four

Listen to some of your favorite music from high school.

*Sing unto him a new song;
play skillfully with a loud noise.*

—Psalm 33:3 KJV

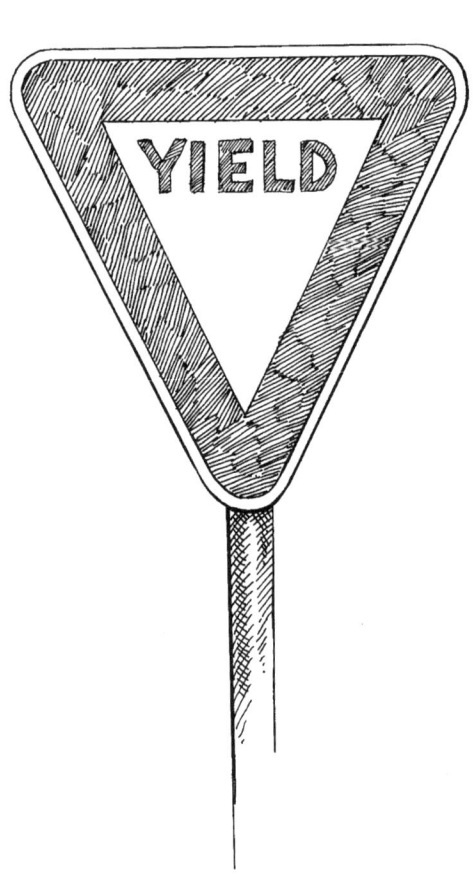

Five

Let another driver cut in front of you in busy traffic.

*Commit thy way unto the L*ORD*; trust also in him; and he shall bring it to pass.*

—Psalm 37:5 KJV

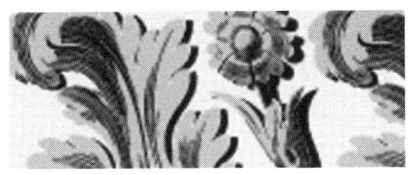

Six

Go antique shopping.

*One generation passeth away,
and another generation cometh:
but the earth abideth for ever.*

—Ecclesiastes 1:4 KJV

Seven

Look for a four-leaf clover.

To every thing there is a season, and a time to every purpose under the heaven.

—Ecclesiastes 3:1 KJV

Eight

Tell a store clerk you appreciate her.

A word fitly spoken is like apples of gold in a setting of silver.

—Proverbs 25:11 NRSV

Nine

Donate a book you've read to the library.

Of making many books there is no end.

—Ecclesiastes 12:12 KJV

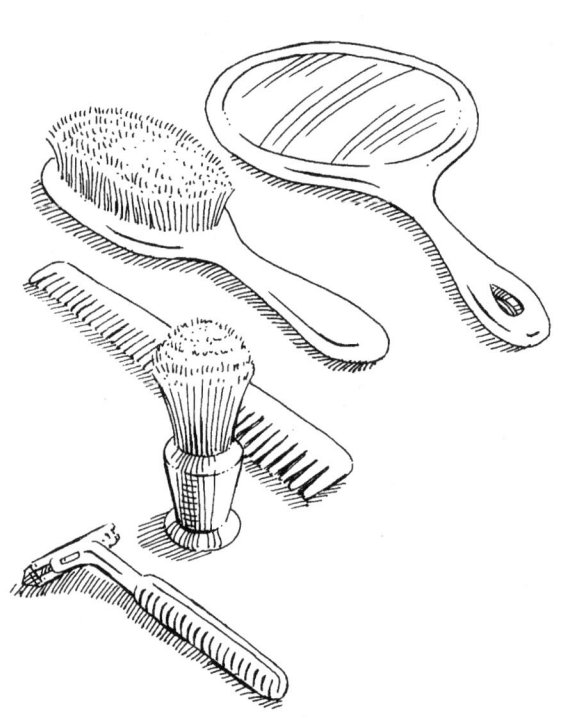

Ten

Tell your husband or significant other how good he looks.

*The heart of her husband trusts in her,
and he will have no lack of gain.*

—Proverbs 31:11 NRSV

Eleven

Make brownies for a neighbor.

~

A *friend loves at all times.*

—Proverbs 17:17 NRSV

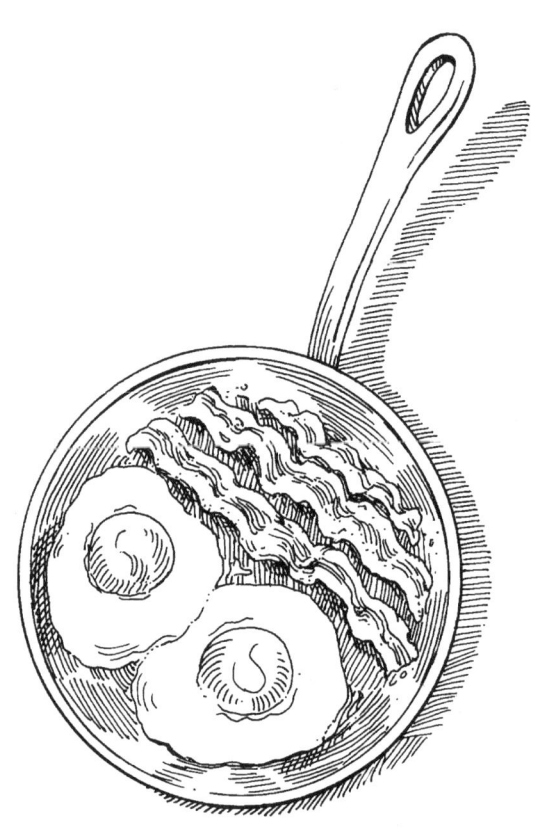

Twelve

Cook breakfast for your supper.

She rises while it is still night and provides food for her household.

—Proverbs 31:15 NRSV

Thirteen

Send a thank-you note to your pastor or someone who has been an inspiration to you.

*I thank my God upon
every remembrance of you.*

—Philippians 1:3 KJV

Fourteen

Make a big pot of coffee and invite a friend or neighbor to share it.

Thou shalt love thy neighbour as thyself.

—Matthew 19:19 KJV

Fifteen

Read a romance novel under a tree.

From the fig tree learn its lesson: as soon as its branch becomes tender and puts forth its leaves, you know that summer is near.

—Matthew 24:32 NRSV

Sixteen

Instead of searching for a gift for someone who seems to have everything, make a donation in the person's name to one of his or her favorite charities.

Freely you have received, freely give.

—Matthew 10:8 NIV

Seventeen

Go to church at a different time or just vary your usual seating. You might meet someone new or gain a new insight.

He put a new song in my mouth, a song of praise to our God.

—Psalm 40:3 NRSV

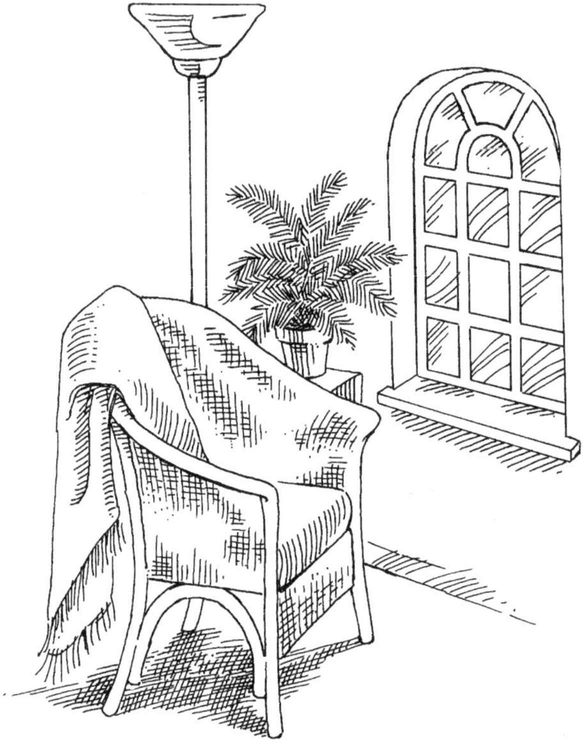

Eighteen

Carve out a little space at home just for you, even if it means turning a chair to face a corner or window. Decorate with a rug, an afghan, a pretty plant, a small table, and good light. Read, plan, or just dream.

My presence shall go with thee, and I will give thee rest.

—Exodus 33:14 KJV

Dear Mrs. Reynolds,

Nineteen

Write a long letter to a favorite high school teacher.

*Happy are those whom you discipline,
O LORD, and whom you teach out of your law.*

—Psalm 94:12 NRSV

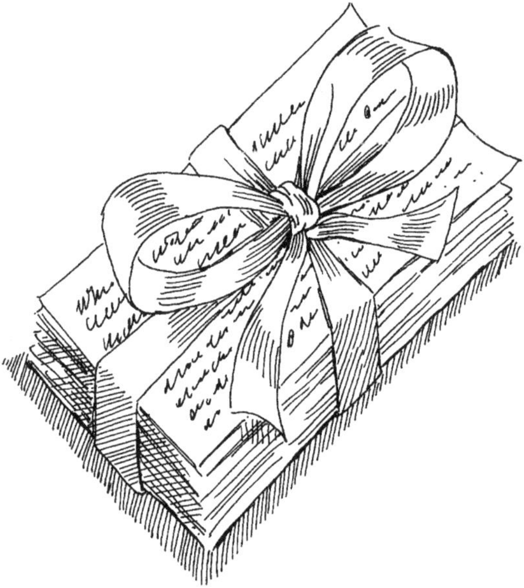

Twenty

Tell your children why you married their father.

I am my beloved's and my beloved is mine.

—Song of Solomon 6:3 NRSV

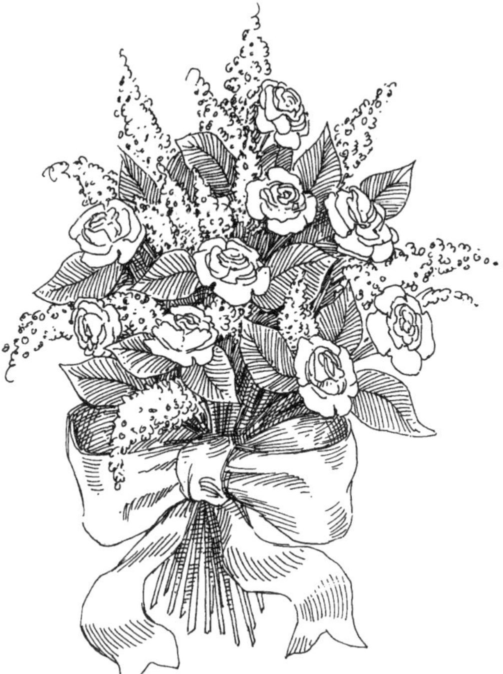

Twenty-one

Buy yourself a bouquet of flowers.

Consider the lilies of the field, how they grow; they toil not, neither do they spin: And yet I say unto you, That even Solomon in all his glory was not arrayed like one of these.

—Matthew 6:28-29 KJV

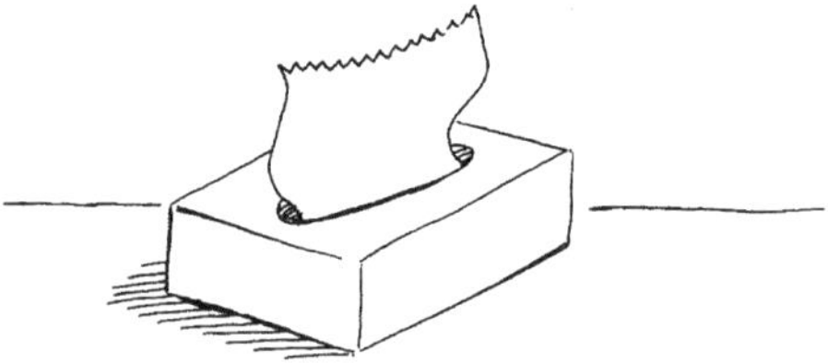

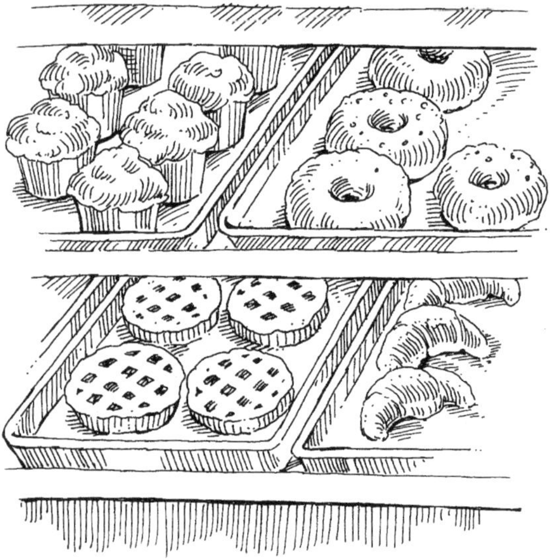

Twenty-two

Take a child to a bakery and let him or her pick out a treat. Buy one for yourself too!

Whoever welcomes one such child in my name welcomes me.

—Matthew 18:5 NRSV

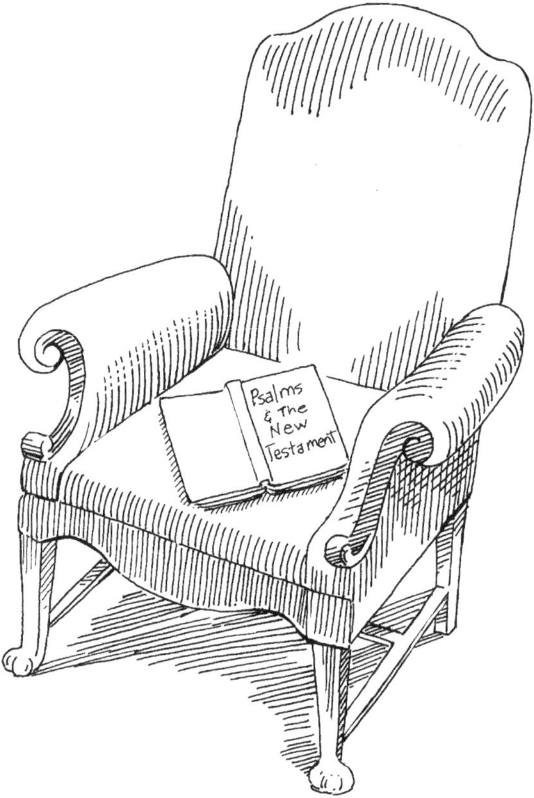
Psalms
& The
New
Testament

Twenty-three

Read Psalm 139.

How precious also are thy thoughts unto me,
O God! how great is the sum of them!

—Psalm 139:16 KJV

Twenty-four

Write or call an old friend you've lost touch with.

Some friends play at friendship but a true friend sticks closer than one's nearest kin.

—Proverbs 18:24 NRSV

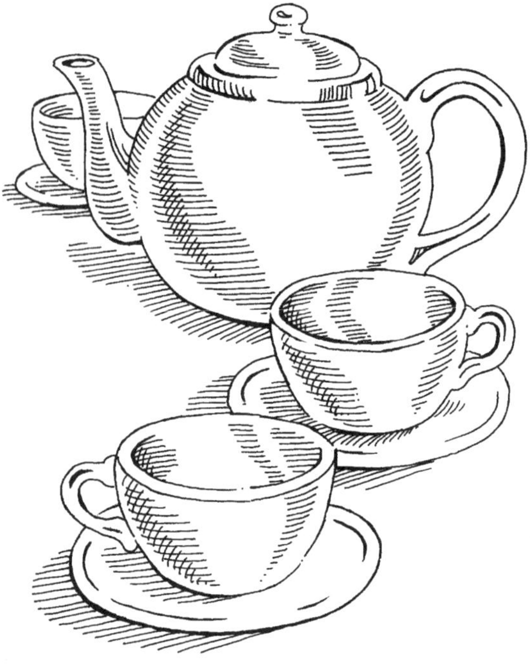

Twenty-five

Plan a night out with one or more friends, or invite your friends over and send the family out.

Suppose a woman has ten silver coins and loses one. . . . When she finds it, she calls her friends and neighbors together and says, "Rejoice with me; I have found my lost coin."

—Luke 15:8-9 NIV

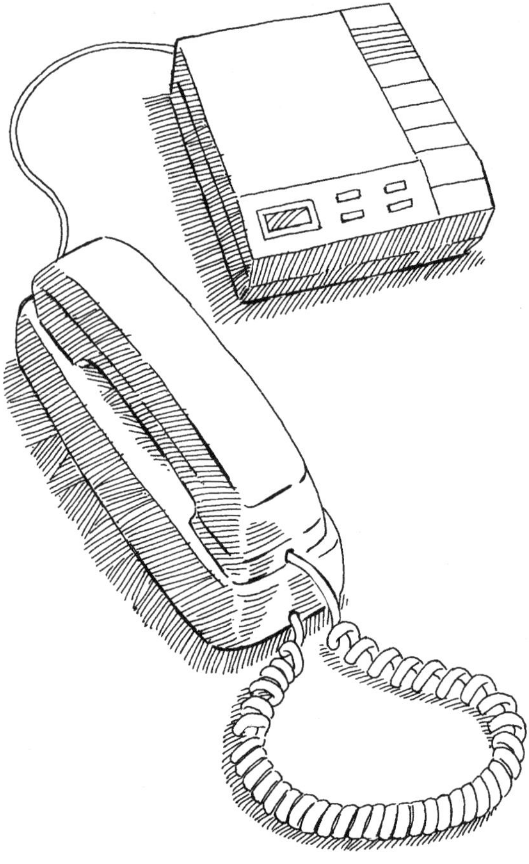

Twenty-six

*L*et the answering machine get the telephone one evening.

To every thing there is a season, and a time to every purpose under the heaven: . . . a time to keep silence, and a time to speak.

—Ecclesiastes 3:1, 7 KJV

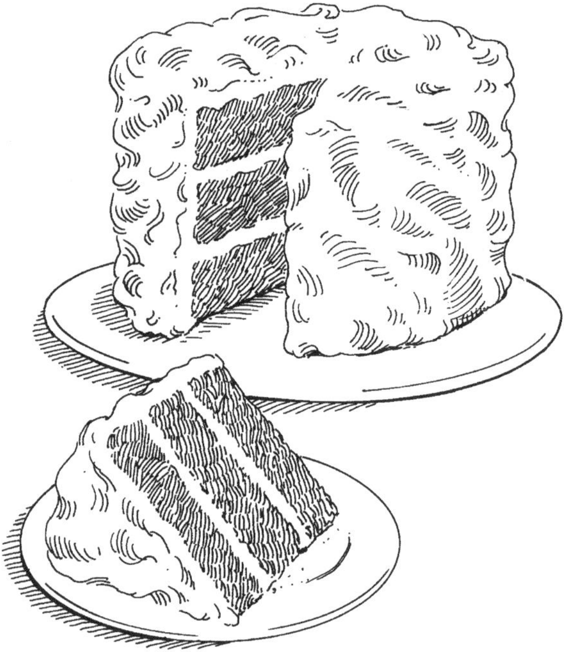

Twenty-seven

Make your favorite dessert.

My child, eat honey, for it is good,
and the drippings of the honeycomb
are sweet to your taste.

—Proverbs 24:13 NRSV

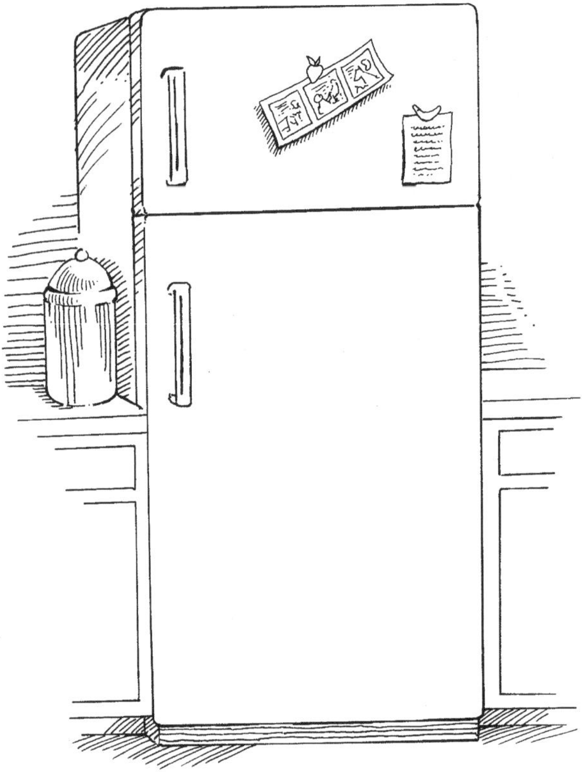

Twenty-eight

*D*isplay a "cartoon of the week" on the refrigerator.

Then was our mouth filled with laughter, and our tongue with singing.

—Psalm 126:2 KJV

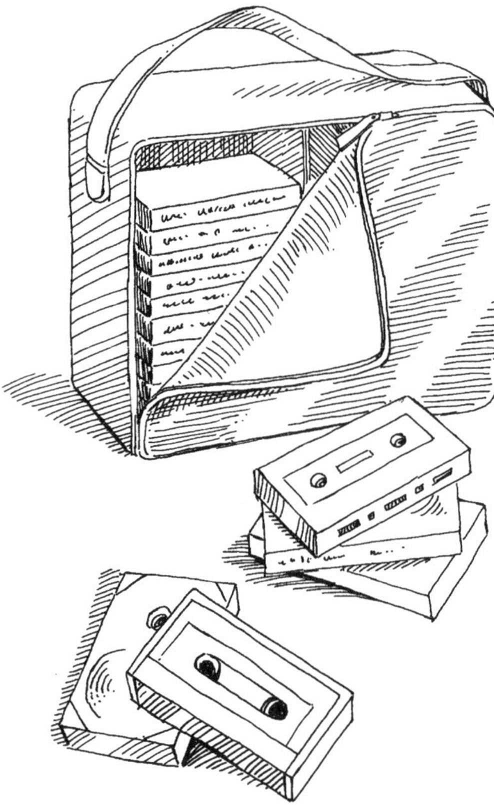

Twenty-nine

*L*isten to a book on tape while driving to work or doing chores.

And he said, "Let anyone with ears to hear listen!"

—Mark 4:9 NRSV

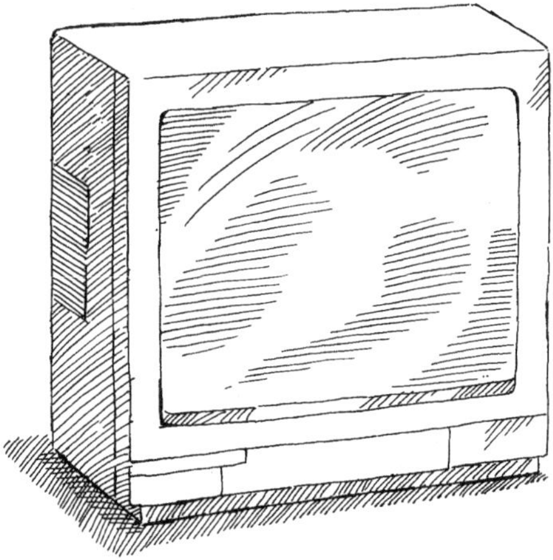

Thirty

Watch cartoons with your husband or another adult friend, and try not to laugh.

He that sitteth in the heavens shall laugh.

—Psalm 2:4 KJV